TO:

FROM:

THE
LEADERSHIP
SECRETS OF
HAMILTON

7 STEPS TO REVOLUTIONARY LEADERSHIP FROM ALEXANDER HAMILTON AND THE FOUNDING FATHERS

GORDON LEIDNER

simple **truths**
▶ Small books. **BIG IMPACT.**

IGNITEREADS
spark impact in just one hour

Published by Simple Truths, an imprint of Sourcebooks, Inc.
P.O. Box 4410, Naperville, Illinois 60567-4410
(630) 961-3900
Fax: (630) 961-2168
sourcebooks.com

Printed and bound in China.
OGP 10 9 8 7 6 5 4 3 2 1

To Jim Martin Jr. of Solutions

A transformational leader

CONTENTS

INTRODUCTION
THE LEADERSHIP SECRETS OF HAMILTON AND THE FOUNDING FATHERS

The Founding Fathers' adoption of the Declaration of Independence, the United States Constitution, and the Bill of Rights was the most revolutionary demonstration of leadership in American political history. Collectively, these documents established the spirit, the letter, and the protection of a radical form of government that was founded not on the rights of kings but on the rights of the common man.

Democracy had been attempted by societies and

city-states at various times in the history of mankind, and it had always failed. But in North America in the late eighteenth century, in spite of the violent resistance of a king who ruled the most powerful nation on earth, democratic government finally succeeded.

What was the primary reason for this success?

It was not because of the political unanimity of the nearly four million colonists in North America. A significant minority of the people, perhaps as much as one third, opposed the establishment of a new nation. It was not because of the strength of the American armies or navy, since they were immensely inferior in numbers, equipment, and weaponry when compared to their foes. It was not because of the wealth and financial independence of the colonies, because the thirteen colonies had fragile economies and were highly dependent on trade with Great Britain.

The key ingredient to the successful establishment of the new nation was leadership—the leadership of a handful of men known today as the *Founding Fathers*.

The Founding Fathers (also called *Founders*) inspired the support and sacrifice of millions of Americans for the cause of establishing an independent, republican form of government. This desire for independence from Great Britain began to take root in the colonies in 1763, shortly after the end of the French and Indian War. To help pay for the standing army he kept in America, Britain's King George III started taxing the colonists. American political activists, who began to call themselves *Patriots*, protested that taxation was unfair because the colonies had no official representation in the British Parliament.

These protests ranged from verbal denunciations in newspapers to violent actions—the latter of which were usually initiated by a Patriot organization known as the *Sons of Liberty*. The king's loyal citizens in America (called *Loyalists* or *Tories*) as well as his appointed governors, jurists, and officials were sometimes the object of harassment or violence. Hoping to avoid bloodshed, the American colonies convened the First Continental Congress in 1774, which appealed to King George III for his intervention. This appeal was ignored, and conflict broke out between American militia and British troops on April 19, 1775, in skirmishes at Lexington and Concord, Massachusetts.

In June of 1775, Congress appointed George Washington commander in chief of the Continental army, and the first major engagement of the war occurred at the Battle of Bunker Hill in Boston. After a year of war, delegates Thomas Jefferson, John Adams, and Benjamin Franklin led the effort to draft the Declaration of Independence, which was signed by the Second Continental Congress on July 4, 1776.

Congress also began drawing up the nation's first constitution in 1776, which became known as the Articles of Confederation. It was a weak document, and went unratified by the states until 1781, but it nevertheless provided some degree of governmental structure until America won the War of Independence in 1783.

Under the Articles of Confederation, Congress had no power of taxation, was wholly dependent on the states for its money, and had no authority to force delinquent states to pay. This resulted in hyperinflation and the nation's being unable to pay its bills. To rectify this, in 1786 Alexander Hamilton introduced a resolution calling for a convention to amend the Articles of Confederation. In response, the Constitutional Convention assembled in Philadelphia in May of 1787. This convention was chaired by George Washington and lasted from May to September of that year. During those eventful months, under the leadership of James Madison, delegates from the states went far beyond the simple amending of the Articles of Confederation, and they drafted a completely new United States Constitution.

The Constitutional Convention of 1787 was held behind closed doors, and the reason for secrecy was the political difficulty of getting fifty-five state representatives to agree on a framework for democratic government. For months the delegates argued about intrinsic issues such as the method of apportioning the House of Representatives, the relationship between state governments and the federal government, and the division of power between the executive, legislative, and judicial branches.

After this prolonged, provocative debate (and what George Washington proclaimed to be a miracle), the delegates signed the Constitution and sent it to the states for ratification. Although this was a huge accomplishment, if it were not for the subsequent leadership of Alexander Hamilton, the proposed constitution would probably not have been ratified. Hamilton, along with James Madison and John Jay, wrote a series of eighty-five articles now known collectively as *The Federalist Papers*. These intellectual arguments in support of the Constitution were essential to its acceptance and ratification by the states, which was completed on June 21, 1788.

In addition to *The Federalist Papers*, there was

another key factor in the successful ratification of the Constitution. Concerned with limiting the power of the federal government and securing the liberty of citizens, many states had refused to ratify the Constitution without the adoption of a bill of rights. Answering this call, James Madison led the development of a series of amendments, ten of which were ratified by the states on December 15, 1791. These first ten amendments to the U.S. Constitution are known today as the Bill of Rights.

After the Constitution was ratified, the Founders realized that it was imperative that the first president of the United States be a man who could unify the young nation. All knew that the first presidential administration would establish important precedents in the areas of finance and foreign relations. George Washington was the only logical choice for president, and his appointments of Alexander Hamilton as secretary of the treasury and Thomas Jefferson as secretary of state proved indispensable to the rapid expansion of the nation.

"But what do we mean by the American Revolution? Do we mean the American war? The Revolution was effected before the war commenced. The Revolution was in the minds and the hearts of the people, a change in their religious sentiments of their duties and obligations... This radical change in the principles, opinions, sentiments, and affections of the people was the real American Revolution."

—JOHN ADAMS[1]

There are a wide range of leadership theories which could be used to analyze the Founding Fathers. Among these are the great man theory, trait theory, behavioral theories, contingency theories, transactional theories, and transformational theories. Although the Founding Fathers individually practiced a broad range of leadership techniques, as a group they are widely recognized today as *transformational* leaders, so the focus will primarily be on this theory.

Transformational leaders are unique in that they motivate followers to make personal sacrifices and go beyond their own self-interests for the good of the larger group. According to James MacGregor Burns, an early contributor to the theory, transformational leadership is a process by which leaders and their followers raise one another to "higher levels of morality and motivation."[ii]

Although there are many variations of transformational leadership theory, most theorists accept Bernard M. Bass's opinion of what a successful transformational leader does. The transformational leader usually inspires followers to feel trust, loyalty, and respect toward him or her. Followers are motivated to do more than they originally expected to do, and they continue to persevere and make sacrifices toward their common goal in spite of personal difficulties or hardship.

Americans faced enormous difficulties and hardships during the Revolutionary War. Whether they were among the freezing, starving soldiers at Valley Forge, the countless young mothers trying to care for their families while their husbands were away, the thousands of farmers who lost everything to the passage of ravenous armies, or the myriad of small businessmen who fell destitute because of hyperinflation and devalued currency, they all contributed to the victory over the king's armies. They not only won the War of American Independence, but they established for themselves and future generations the first successful, as well as only surviving, democratic government on earth.

The modern-day leader may not have a task as monumental as the one that faced the Founding Fathers. However, the principles the Founders followed are still useful for various modern leadership challenges such as the establishment of a new company, the rejuvenation of a failing business, and the motivation of an uninspired workforce.

This book explores seven leadership secrets of selected Founding Fathers (Hamilton, Washington, Jefferson, Madison, Adams, Henry, and Franklin). Most of the leadership skills examined are taken from transformational leadership theory. Each chapter begins with a historical event that illustrates how one or more of the Founding Fathers used the discussed leadership skill. The chapters, which are generally presented in order of historical occurrence, are as follows:

1. Prepare Yourself
2. Exemplify Moral Integrity
3. Go Beyond Self-Interest
4. Establish Clear Goals
5. Respect Your People
6. Convey an Inspiring Vision
7. Be a Mentor

Each leadership secret is supported by three key actions for success that can be employed today.

1

PREPARE YOURSELF

Of all the Founding Fathers, Alexander Hamilton stands out as the one who began life with the fewest prospects for success. Most of the Founders were raised in either stable or advantaged families in the American colonies; Hamilton was born out of wedlock, raised in the West Indies, and orphaned at thirteen years of age.

The year of Hamilton's birth is uncertain, but most historians now believe it was 1755. When Alexander was four years old, his mother, Rachel, was abandoned by her common-law husband James Hamilton, who claimed she was an adulteress. Rachel Hamilton did the best she could to provide for Alexander and his brother, James, but she would probably have failed if it had not been for some financial aid from relatives. She managed a general store out of the first floor of her home on the island of St. Croix and lived with her sons on the second floor. Because of the accusations of her former husband, she and her children were at a social disadvantage in the tiny island community, and young Alexander was forced to receive much of his education from a tutor or self-study at home rather than from the church. A life of hardship for young Alexander was further punctuated with tragedy when his mother died of a virulent fever in 1768.

Without close relatives to adopt them, Alexander and his brother were separated. James became apprenticed to a carpenter, and Alexander had the good fortune of being taken in by a local merchant named Thomas Stevens.

At the age of fourteen, Hamilton became a clerk

at a local import-export firm, Beekman and Cruger, which traded various goods such as livestock, building materials, and perishable commodities. As a clerk, Hamilton learned all aspects of the business, including accounts management, inventory, and the conversion of foreign currencies. His employers discovered that he had a keen mind for trade and global commerce. By the age of seventeen, he was put completely in charge of the business for months when the owner put out to sea.

When not clerking, Hamilton voraciously devoured books on a wide variety of subjects, which included theology and the Greek and Roman classics. He wrote poetry, some of which was published in a local newspaper, the *Royal Danish American Gazette*. Finally, Hamilton's self-education paid off when St. Croix was devastated in 1772 by a powerful hurricane, which inspired him to write an article for the *Gazette*. This human-interest story was written "with such verve and gusto"[i] that municipal leaders decided this talented, amiable youth should be given an opportunity to improve himself. They pooled their resources and sent Alexander Hamilton to New York to pursue a college education.

Upon arriving in New York, Hamilton immediately enrolled in a preparatory school to begin last-minute cramming in subjects such as mathematics, Greek, and Latin. He studied incessantly, and he so impressed his educators that he was enrolled in King's College (now Columbia University) in 1773 as a *private student*, and was formally matriculated in 1774.

At King's College, Hamilton's powerful mind, exceptional work ethic, and agreeable personality soon earned him the respect and friendship of both peers and professors. King's College was a bastion of Loyalists, and Hamilton was initially sympathetic to their cause, but he soon found himself agreeing with those who advocated American independence. He published two popular pamphlets that supported the actions of the Sons of Liberty. He supplemented his

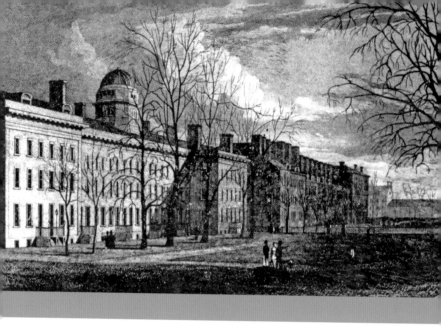

academic pursuits with studies in the military arts, and after the first shots of the rebellion were fired in 1775, Hamilton joined a New York volunteer militia company.

~~~~~~~~

Three key actions for preparing yourself

☞ Recognize Your Challenges

☞ Set Personal Goals

☞ Never Give Up

RECOGNIZE YOUR CHALLENGES

As Alexander Hamilton would have realized, the ancient Greek aphorism *know thyself* is an excellent place to start in the study of leadership. There are all kinds of advice on how you can stand out from the crowd, impress your boss, and climb the corporate ladder. But you are unique, so it is important to first examine yourself in order to recognize what your strengths and weaknesses are.

There are many practical ways to assess your particular skills and challenges. Read about strong leaders and compare yourself to them. Take online personality tests and skills assessments. Consider part-time work in fields that are related to what you are interested in.

Ask your friends what they think your challenges are—and don't take offense at their responses! Ask your boss, mentors, and coworkers. And don't forget the one who probably knows you better than anyone else. Ask Mom!

"No reflection ought to be made on any man on account of birth, provided that his manners rise decently with his circumstances, and that he affects not to forget the level he came from; when he does, he ought to be led back and shown the mortifying picture of originality."

—THOMAS PAINE[II]

SET PERSONAL GOALS

In addition to the assessment of your strengths and weaknesses, *knowing thyself* should include an assessment of your lifetime dreams. Most people have lifetime dreams, but they remain only dreams— dreams that never become goals. To turn your dreams into reality you must set up both long-term and short-term goals.

To fulfill your dream, you will have to establish multiple long-term goals that complement one another. For instance, perhaps you have the dream of being an engineer. It's obvious that the engineer dream can be defined as a *career* goal. But you need more than a career goal to attain this dream—you need to determine which associated long-term goals support it (for example, educational goals, financial goals, family goals).

Once you have set your long-term goals, start setting short-term goals that will help you attain them. You can decide how short the short-term goals are, but a common duration is five years. After five-year goals are established, set up smaller and smaller goals that will help you reach your five-year goals. The small goals should be very short, such as completing a class or perhaps even reading a specific book. Remember that each goal should always support achievement of the higher goal.

"I must study politics and war that my sons may have liberty to study mathematics and philosophy. My sons ought to study mathematics and philosophy...in order to give their children a right to study painting, poetry, music, architecture, statuary, tapestry, and porcelain."

—JOHN ADAMS[III]

NEVER GIVE UP

Even if everyone else abandons you, it is imperative that you never give up on yourself. So what if you miss that promotion or aren't appointed to that leadership position you thought was so important? There is always another promotion to pursue, another team you can join, or another company you can switch to.

The following is an excerpt from the earliest surviving letter by Alexander Hamilton, written in 1769. It is a stellar example of a young man who, although he wasn't certain what he was going to do with his life, was resolved to never give up on himself. At that time, his society saw him as little more than an orphaned, illegitimately-born, fourteen-year-old clerk. In this letter, he is writing to his good friend Edward (Ned) Stevens, who had moved to New York to go to college. Hamilton laments his current station in life and hopes to someday improve upon it. He believed that his most likely means of advancement one day would be as a soldier and expressed his hope for war.

Ned, my Ambition is prevalent that I contemn the grov'ling and condition of a Clerk or the like, to which my Fortune &c. condemns me and would willingly risk my life tho' not my Character to exalt my Station. Im confident, Ned that my Youth excludes me from any hopes of immediate Preferment nor do I desire it, but I mean to prepare the way for futurity. Im no Philosopher you see and may

be jus[t]ly said to Build Castles in the Air. My Folly makes me ashamd and beg youll Conceal it, yet Neddy we have seen such Schemes successfull when the Projector is Constant I shall Conclude saying I wish there was a War.

I am, Dr. Edward, yours, Alex Hamilton.[iv]

"Perseverance and spirit have done wonders in all ages."

—GEORGE WASHINGTON[v]

BIOGRAPHICAL NOTE
ALEXANDER HAMILTON

....

Alexander Hamilton, born on the Caribbean island of Nevis and raised on St. Croix, was orphaned at the age of thirteen. Through hard work and self-directed study, Hamilton won the respect of community leaders, and through their generosity, he was sent to New York at the age of seventeen to pursue a college education. While in college, he was caught up in the spirit of the revolution and joined a New York militia company. As a young captain of artillery, his courage and talents were soon recognized by General George Washington, who appointed him to his personal staff. In his service to Washington as a trusted liaison officer, Hamilton proved invaluable. After the war, Hamilton's political leadership was essential to the ratification of the U.S. Constitution. When Washington was elected the first president of the United States, he appointed the thirty-four-year-old Hamilton to be the nation's first secretary of the treasury. In this capacity, Hamilton's brilliant mind was well employed, and he soon improved the faltering American economy. He founded America's first native polit-ical party, the Federalists. He had an aristocratic leadership style, and his passionate arguments with peers earned him many enemies, including Thomas Jefferson, John Adams, and Aaron Burr. In 1804, Hamilton was shot and killed in a duel by Vice President Aaron Burr, leaving behind him a remarkable legacy at the age of only forty-nine.

2

EXEMPLIFY MORAL INTEGRITY

During the American Revolutionary War, George Washington was given the most difficult task of all the Founding Fathers when the Continental Congress commissioned him as commander in chief of the Continental army on June 19, 1775. His duty was to fight the occupying armies of Great Britain—the most powerful military force on earth—and somehow win victory in the face of nearly impossible odds.

The British had stationed in the colonies large,

well-disciplined armies of professional soldiers led by battle-hardened officers. Washington, on the other hand, had much smaller, loosely organized forces that consisted of poorly trained militia and unreliable volunteers. The British army had a well-organized system of logistics that could deliver ample supplies of ammunition and food, backed by a strong navy that could provide rapid transport. Washington had to count on whatever supplies could be conjured up by a powerless Congress, small businessmen, and local farmers. The British were well-provisioned in their immaculate red uniforms, well-stocked knapsacks, and fine boots. But in Washington's army, uniforms and warm clothing were a scarce commodity, even among his field officers, and many of his men went barefoot. The British officer corps was well-trained, highly disciplined, and proficient in the art of war. Most of Washington's officer corps had no formal training, little regard for discipline, and had never led men in battle.

Why was George Washington chosen to be the leader of this "rabble-in-arms"[i]?

There were several obvious reasons, such as the combat experience he had gained during the French and Indian War. Fighting on the side of the British in that conflict, he became a capable officer who demonstrated admirable leadership skills in battle. Washington was also an influential resident from the important colony of Virginia and the wealthy owner of a large tobacco plantation. Although these were important reasons, the young nation needed more than this to put its fate in Washington's hands.

More than any other leader of his time, George Washington was recognized as a person of unquestioned moral integrity. He was universally acknowledged as someone who was honest, trustworthy, forbearing, and of sound judgment. These character traits made him "the unanimous choice" of Congress for the critical role of commander in chief of the Continental army. Although political leaders such as Thomas Jefferson,

John Adams, and Benjamin Franklin would later give the new nation the inspiring vision defined in the Declaration of Independence, they discerned that for now, in time of war, it was the army that would decide America's future. Knowing that Congress could provide the army little in the way of supplies or wages, they recognized it was of ultimate importance that the soldiers have a respected commander to follow. "The liberties of America depend upon him," wrote John Adams, shortly after Washington's appointment to command.[ii]

Although Washington was the primary example of a leader with moral integrity, he was by no means the only one. General Washington demanded excellence from his subordinates, and he promoted a young officer by the name of Alexander Hamilton to aide-de-camp. Hamilton had demonstrated to Washington not only moral integrity, but also diplomacy, industry, and genius. As a key staff officer, Hamilton participated in strategic planning sessions, acted as Washington's representative in important meetings,

maintained critical communications with Congress, and signed important documents on Washington's behalf. Washington's trust of Hamilton would continue throughout the war and into his presidency.

Three key actions for moral integrity

☞ Be Honest with Your Followers

☞ Admit Your Own Weaknesses

☞ Develop an Environment of Trust

BE HONEST WITH YOUR FOLLOWERS

"Honesty," President George Washington said in his Farewell Address, "is always the best policy."

Common sense will tell you that no one wants to work for someone who does not tell the truth. After all, if you can't trust your boss, what's the use of counting on that next raise the boss says you will receive? Can you count on that promised bonus or promotion? When the boss says you did a great job—is it sincere? Is your job secure? Lack of honesty in a leader quickly degenerates into a lack of trust, increased skepticism, and the loss of commitment on the part of followers.

The leadership action addressed in Chapter Four, "Provide Meaningful Guidance," shows one way your honesty can directly benefit your team and followers.

> **"The first of qualities for a great statesman is to be honest."**
>
> **—JOHN ADAMS**[III]

ADMIT YOUR OWN WEAKNESSES

Weak leaders often believe that admitting they are wrong is a sign of poor leadership. Don't fall into that trap! If you refuse to admit your own weaknesses or mistakes, you will find yourself continually defending your poor choices and taking your followers down a path that is second best—or worse. To hide your mistakes, you may end up placing unfair blame on others in order to prove you were right.

Being afraid to admit your own weakness is actually

a form of dishonesty, and dishonesty, once discovered, breeds contempt. If you are weak in a certain leadership or technical skill, chances are that your people already know it or will soon discover it. By admitting your weakness to subordinates, you are honoring them. They will realize that they have your confidence and recognize their opportunity to be of greater service to you. Opening up with your followers and asking them to help you increases trust and conveys a sense of personal worth to everyone.

"Cherish, therefore, the spirit of our people, and keep alive their attention. Do not be too severe upon their errors, but reclaim them by enlightening them. If once they become inattentive to the public affairs, you and I, and Congress, and assemblies, judges, and governors, shall all become wolves."

——THOMAS JEFFERSON[IV]

"It is of great importance to set a resolution, not to be shaken, never to tell an untruth. There is no vice so mean, so pitiful, so contemptible; and he who permits himself to tell a lie once, finds it much easier to do it a second and a third time, till at length it becomes habitual; he tells lies without attending to it, and truths without the world's believing him. This falsehood of the tongue leads to that of the heart, and in time depraves all its good dispositions."

—THOMAS JEFFERSON[v]

DEVELOP AN ENVIRONMENT OF TRUST

Developing an environment of trust is an effective means of increasing collaboration and leadership skills in teams. To increase the environment of trust, you must start with yourself. Tell your team what your personal commitments (as a leader) are, and pledge to keep them. Ask your followers to hold you accountable. Challenge them to come to you with any concerns about your leadership or about the organization's performance in respect to company business goals.

Do not blame or punish followers when they make mistakes, but encourage them to learn from them. Praise your followers when they identify problems, and help them to develop solutions.

Once your followers believe that you trust them, your behavior will bring out the best in your team members and your organization will perform at increasingly higher levels of trust and collaboration.

"In every nomination to office I have endeavored, as far as my own knowledge extended, or information could be obtained, to make fitness of character my primary object."

—GEORGE WASHINGTON[VI]

CONSTITUTIONAL CONVENTION
ENVIRONMENT OF TRUST

◇◇◇◇◇◇◇◇◇◇◇◇◇◇◇◇◇◇

In 1787, four years after the Revolutionary War ended, delegates from twelve states convened in Philadelphia for the purpose of amending the Articles of Confederation. Realizing the significance of the event, they decided to meet in the same room of the State House where the Declaration of Independence had been signed in 1776. Once assembled, they almost immediately agreed that what the nation needed most was a completely new constitution rather than an amended one.

Appreciating the difficulty of the task before them, they knew that their deliberations must be done in secret. This was because of potential outside interference by lobbyists and the press. Lobbyists, worried that their own special interests might be harmed by the outcome of the convention, were anxious to influence the discussions. Members of the press were eager to publish daily details of the debates and sell newspapers. So the delegates decided to impose on themselves a gag order, to which they all swore adherence.

They posted armed sentries outside of the doors so that no outsiders could interfere, established some basic parliamentary rules, and chose the most respected man in the country, George Washington, to preside over the convention. Having established this environment of trust, over the next four months the fifty-five delegates proceeded to debate, draft, and approve a new constitution.

WASHINGTON'S HONESTY

◇◇◇◇◇◇◇◇◇◇◇◇◇◇◇◇

Legend has it that six-year-old George Washington received a hatchet as a gift and cut down his father's cherry tree. When his father discovered what he had done, he became angry and confronted him. Young George bravely said, "I cannot tell a lie… I cut it with my hatchet." Rather than becoming angry, Washington's father embraced him and rejoiced because he considered his son's honesty to be worth more than a thousand trees.

We know today that this story is a myth, invented by one of Washington's earliest biographers, Mason Locke Weems. But even myths have their value. As a child, future President of the United States Abraham Lincoln read Weems's biography of Washington and was deeply impressed by the first president's moral integrity. Lincoln became a lifelong admirer of Washington, and he earned the sobriquet "Honest Abe" long before he became president.

BIOGRAPHICAL NOTE
GEORGE WASHINGTON

....

George Washington, a wealthy member of Virginia's planter class, started his military career as an officer of American militia troops in the British army during the French and Indian War. A man of innumerable qualities, including moral integrity, tact, and patience, he was by far the most popular and respected American of his day. Soon after the American Revolution began, he was commissioned commander in chief of the Continental army and served the nation in this capacity throughout the entire eight years of war. He was selected to preside at the Constitutional Convention in 1787, and after the Constitution was ratified, he was chosen as the first president of the United States. He was president for two terms, from 1789 to 1797. Although he never formally aligned himself with a political party, he was philosophically closest to Federalist Party policies and frequently sided with his secretary of the treasury, Alexander Hamilton, on economic and leadership issues. Washington sought balance and harmony within his cabinet, but the increasing rancor between Thomas Jefferson and Alexander Hamilton made this increasingly difficult. Washington saw Jefferson's criticism of his administration's fiscal policies as disruptive, and Jefferson did not serve in the second Washington administration.

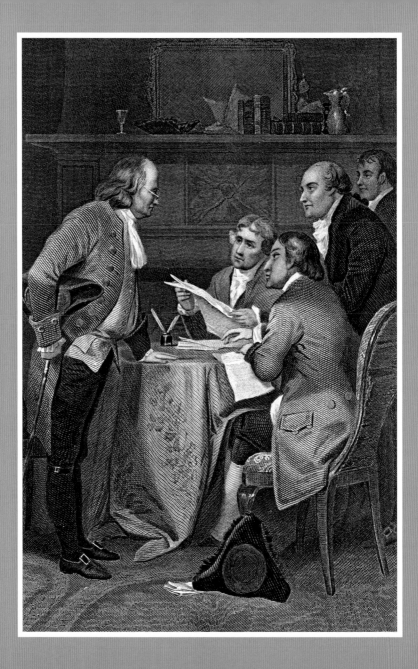

3

GO BEYOND SELF-INTEREST

"We hold these truths to be self-evident, that all men are created equal, that they are endowed by their Creator with certain unalienable rights, that among these are Life, Liberty and the pursuit of Happiness—That to secure these rights, Governments are instituted among Men, deriving their just powers from the consent of the governed,—That whenever any Form of Government becomes destructive of these

ends, it is the Right of the People to alter or to abolish it, and to institute new Government…"

—DECLARATION OF INDEPENDENCE

With this iconic statement from the Preamble of the Declaration of Independence, the Founding Fathers began their justification for the establishment of an independent nation. In this pronouncement, the Founders fully realized the significance of what they were doing and the danger they were getting themselves into. They were rebelling against Great Britain's monarch, the most powerful ruler on earth, and they knew that King George III would see their actions as treason—punishable by death.

To justify a declaration of independence from Great Britain, the Founding Fathers offered a moral argument that few people of their day would have disagreed with. Their argument was that the right to life, liberty, and the pursuit of happiness was granted by the creator of the universe himself. It was therefore their duty, as God-fearing men, to abolish their ties to the king and establish a new government. By acknowledging their duty, and putting their lives at risk in support of the Declaration of Independence, they were placing the interests of millions of Americans ahead of their own.

After the Preamble in the Declaration, the Founders continued with an indictment of the king, describing his actions toward the American colonists. They announced that the king was not treating them equally with the people in Great Britain. He offered them no representation in Parliament. He taxed them without redress. He forced them to quarter troops within their homes. They listed a total of twenty-seven grievances.

When they finished, the primary authors of the Declaration of Independence—Thomas Jefferson, John Adams, Benjamin Franklin, and two others— submitted their pronouncement to the Second Continental Congress for its approval. Over the ensuing weeks, a total of fifty-six representatives of the Second Continental Congress risked their lives by signing the Declaration of Independence. Benjamin Franklin, the oldest and some would say the wisest of the delegates, purportedly quipped that "we must indeed all hang together, or most assuredly we shall all hang separately."[i]

The Declaration of Independence was put into print and displayed in towns and villages throughout the thirteen colonies. It was read by soldiers on their way to battle, civilians on their way to work—everyone who wondered why their leaders were taking them into harm's way. The willingness of the Founders to put themselves in jeopardy inspired millions of others to endure their own hardships and sacrifices in the war—for the purpose of forming a new nation that was founded on the principle that "all men are created equal."

~~~~~~~~

Three key secrets for going beyond self-interest

☞ Define What Is Most Important

☞ Develop a Plan for Change

☞ Demonstrate Your Personal Commitment

DEFINE WHAT IS MOST IMPORTANT

With the Declaration of Independence, the Founders described what they believed was wrong with the actions of the British government and what should be done about it.

Although your leadership task will not be as large as the overthrow of a national government, it is still important. Perhaps your organization's goals are no longer relevant and need to be changed. Maybe you've discovered that your company's business practices are unethical. Perhaps you've recognized that a product needs to be developed to solve an important customer problem.

As the leader, you must state the problem clearly, and justify your proposed actions to followers. If the work will require self-sacrifice on your followers' part, you must show them why it is important enough for their commitment. Transformational leaders inspire followers to get in the game because *it's the right thing to do.*

"The hour is fast approaching on which the honor and success of this army, and the safety of our bleeding country, depend. Remember, officers and soldiers, that you are freemen fighting for the blessings of liberty—that slavery will be your portion... if you do not acquit yourselves like men."

—GEORGE WASHINGTON[11]

DEVELOP A PLAN FOR CHANGE

In the Declaration of Independence, the Founders did not begin with a list of what the king was doing wrong. They began by stating what was morally right and then followed up with their list of the king's errors. They then offered a high-level plan for solution—which was the establishment of a new nation.

Plans are usually developed after a vision is conveyed (Chapter Six) and clear goals are established (Chapter Four). Your plan should be practical. It should be achievable. It should be something that all of your followers can recognize as beneficial. You should clearly describe who will benefit—such as other parts of the organization, or clients, or future employees.

"This was the object of the Declaration of Independence. Not to find out new principles, or new arguments, never before thought of, not merely to say things which had never been said before; but to place before mankind the common sense of the subject, in terms so plain and firm as to command their assent, and to justify ourselves in the independent stand we were compelled to take."

—THOMAS JEFFERSON[iii]

DEMONSTRATE YOUR PERSONAL COMMITMENT

The Founding Fathers put their skin in the game! In signing their names to the Declaration, they were accepting the risk of prosecution for treason. Their courage was an example to millions of people in the colonies.

Likewise, you must demonstrate to your followers your own commitment to the plan. If they can see that you are willing to take risks, it will incentivize them to do the same. The best way to demonstrate your personal commitment is by publicly communicating to the organization what your personal roles, responsibilities, and goals will be. Tell your followers what you will deliver and ask them to hold you accountable. Make certain your goals are measurable, and present your progress against goals at scheduled meetings. Encourage your followers to provide feedback at these meetings, and be ready to answer their questions about the team's progress as the plan develops.

"For the support of this Declaration, with a firm reliance on the protection of Divine Providence, we mutually pledge to each other our Lives, our Fortunes, and our sacred Honor."

—DECLARATION OF INDEPENDENCE

HAMILTON'S COMMITMENT

◇◇◇◇◇◇◇◇◇◇◇◇◇◇◇◇◇◇

After Alexander Hamilton was promoted from a captain of artillery to lieutenant colonel on Washington's staff, he spent most of the war behind the lines and away from danger. He desperately wanted to prove once again in battle his commitment to the cause of American independence, but Washington was reluctant to lose the services of this talented officer. Finally, shortly before the last major battle of the war, Washington relented and gave Hamilton command of a light infantry battalion. On the evening of October 14, 1781, Hamilton and his men were given the task of taking Redoubt No. 10, a fortification on the outer lines of the British army besieged at Yorktown. Hamilton wanted to take the enemy fort by surprise, so he had his men unload their muskets in order to prevent accidental discharge, fix bayonets, and assemble for the assault. At eight o'clock, the signal—three successive shells— burst overhead, and Hamilton and his men ran fearlessly toward their enemy. Shouting "Rochambeau!" as their watchword, Hamilton and his soldiers clambered over the parapets. Within ten minutes they had taken the fort, at the cost of only eight Americans killed. The loss of this fort, along with another redoubt taken simultaneously by French soldiers, proved to be the last straw for the British commander General Cornwallis. He surrendered his entire army within five days. Hamilton, the brave young officer who was at last given battle command, was hailed as a hero in the last fight of the last major battle of the war.

BIOGRAPHICAL NOTE
THOMAS JEFFERSON

....

The owner of a large plantation in Virginia, Thomas Jefferson is widely acknowledged as the principal author of the Declaration of Independence. He was also a member of the Continental Congress, secretary of state in the Washington administration, a diplomat to France who helped negotiate the Treaty of Paris, and the third president of the United States. As a large plantation owner, he diligently pursued interests in science, invention, farming, architecture, political science, religion, and philosophy. He established the Democratic-Republican Party in 1791, and was a strong advocate of an agrarian-centric national economy and a less centralized national government. This, along with other philosophical differences such as Jefferson's support of slavery, brought him into frequent conflict with the leader of the Federalist Party and the secretary of the treasury Alexander Hamilton. Both men were highly capable, intelligent leaders, and their conflicting philosophies were the primary reason for the establishment of the two-party political system in America.

4

ESTABLISH CLEAR GOALS

In September of 1786, the United States of America was in trouble. Although it had won its independence from Great Britain at the Treaty of Paris on September 3, 1783, the world's newest sovereign nation was in danger of falling apart. Its constitution, known as the Articles of Confederation, provided for no executive officer, no system of national courts, no means of raising revenue, no authority to control or regulate trade, and no power to compel states to follow the laws.

From September 11 to 14, 1786, a dozen commissioners from the states of Virginia, Delaware, Pennsylvania, New Jersey, and New York met in convention at Annapolis, Maryland. At this convention, Alexander Hamilton introduced a resolution that he proposed sending to their respective state legislatures. The resolution asked the states to send delegates to Philadelphia in May of the following year for the goal of "[taking] into consideration the situation of the United States, to devise such further provisions as shall appear to them necessary to render the constitution of the Federal Government adequate to the exigencies of the Union…"[i]

As a result of the Annapolis Convention, twelve of the thirteen states committed to sending delegates to Philadelphia, and a quorum of state delegates assembled there on May 25, 1787. Knowing Washington's leadership was essential, Hamilton convinced the reluctant hero to preside over the assembly. Although the purpose of the convention was ostensibly to simply amend the Articles of Confederation, Federalist leaders Alexander Hamilton and James Madison intended to do much more. Madison brought with him a blueprint for a completely new government charter and led the effort to debate and adopt the new constitution. It took four months of intense discussions behind locked doors, but on September 17, 1787, the document was signed by thirty-nine of the fifty-five delegates and sent to the states for ratification.

Although brilliantly conceived and ably written, the Constitution was little more than ink on paper until it was ratified by three-fourths of the states. Over the course of the ensuing nine months, Hamilton and Madison would find the ratification of their proposed constitution seriously impeded by Anti-Federalists such as Patrick Henry, Samuel Adams, and George Mason.

Having set the goal at the Annapolis Convention to improve or replace the Articles of Confederation, Alexander Hamilton now led the effort for the new constitution's successful ratification by the states.

He recruited fellow Federalists James Madison and John Jay to assist him in writing a series of what today would be called op-ed articles. Published in several newspapers, these articles provided highly persuasive intellectual and political arguments for the passage and defense of the Constitution. Hamilton set a feverish pace for himself and his two compatriots and produced the articles so quickly that the Anti-Federalists were overwhelmed. The commentaries averaged two thousand words in length and were generated at the pace of from two to four articles a week beginning in October of 1787. In all, eighty-five were written, and today they are collectively known as *The Federalist Papers*.

The Federalist Papers were indispensable to the goal of the successful ratification of the United States Constitution, which took place on June 21, 1788. Additionally, *The Federalist Papers* have become an invaluable resource for judicial bodies such as the United States Supreme Court in cases where the intention of the Founding Fathers is required for juris-dictional decisions.

Three key actions to establish clear goals

☞ Define a Challenging Team Goal

☞ Show Everyone How to Contribute

☞ Provide Meaningful Guidance

DEFINE A CHALLENGING TEAM GOAL

As a leader, you will need to establish goals at multiple levels (for yourself, your team, and your followers), but you should start by establishing a challenging team goal. This is because both your goals as a leader and your followers' goals should always support the goal of the larger group or team.

A challenging team goal might be improbable, but it should not be impossible. If your followers perceive that the team goal is not realistic or achievable, it will be difficult to get their buy-in or their ideas of ways they could successfully contribute. To demonstrate that your team goal is realistic, provide details on how it will be achieved. Tell them what resources will be available. Show the schedule and subtasks. Demonstrate not only your own commitment, but—if possible—the commitment of upper management as well.

"In framing a government which is to be administered by men over men, the great difficulty lies in this: you must first enable the government to control the governed; and in the next place oblige it to control itself."

—JAMES MADISON[11]

SHOW EVERYONE HOW TO CONTRIBUTE

After defining the team goal, you should explain to your followers how they can individually contribute to the accomplishment of that goal. This is best done by helping them establish personal project goals that contribute to the team goal, facilitating their progress toward accomplishment of their goals, and celebrating their success.

To come up with effective project goals for followers, you must not only consider their educational background, job maturity, and job skills, but also their personal career goals. Once you and your followers have developed their project goals, it is extremely important that you demonstrate your commitment to their success. Finally, when the project is over, acknowledge how well everyone did toward not only the team goal but their individual project goals as well.

"It seems to have been reserved to the people of this country, by their conduct and example, to decide the important question, whether societies of men are really capable or not of establishing good government from reflection and choice, or whether they are forever destined to depend, for their political constitutions, on accident and force."

—ALEXANDER HAMILTON[III]

PROVIDE MEANINGFUL GUIDANCE

Leadership theorists used to talk a lot about providing good feedback to followers. A more commonly used term today is to provide guidance, and a popular methodology is to use *radical candor*. The idea of radical candor is to ignore the old adage that "if you can't say something nice about a person, don't say anything at all" and instead say what you really think people need to hear in order to improve themselves or meet the team goal. To be helpful, this has to be done with the followers' best interest in mind. If you don't truly care about your followers, your candid advice on improvement will be neither accepted nor effective.

Once you have established a clear team goal, shown everyone how they can contribute, and provided guidance for team members on how to best improve their work, the goals you set for the present and the future will be crystal clear.

"I think the best way of doing good to the poor is not making them easy *in* poverty, but leading or driving them *out* of it. In my youth I traveled much, and I observed in different countries that the more public provisions were made for the poor, the less they provided for themselves, and of course became poorer. And, on the contrary, the less was done for them, the more they did for themselves, and became richer."

—BENJAMIN FRANKLIN[IV]

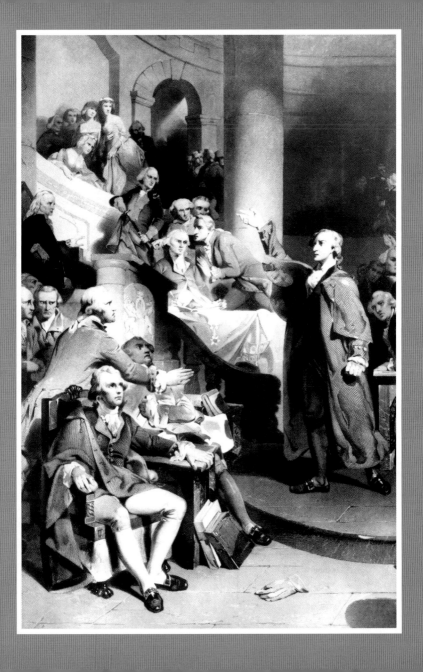

BIOGRAPHICAL NOTE
PATRICK HENRY

....

Patrick Henry was an attorney, politician, and wealthy plantation owner from Virginia. As one of the earliest Founding Fathers to promote independence from Britain, he introduced in 1765 the Virginia Stamp Act Resolutions, which are sometimes credited with being a catalyst to the Revolutionary War ten years later. When the war loomed near, Henry inspired the Virginia

House of Burgesses to enroll a militia unit for the colony's defense with his "Give me liberty or give me death!" speech. He was commissioned as a colonel in the First Virginia Regiment. After the war, Henry served two terms as governor of Virginia, which was his highest political office. A staunch Anti-Federalist and proponent of states' rights, Henry opposed the adoption of the U.S. Constitution because he thought it gave too much power to the federal government. Concerned for the rights of individuals, he joined Madison in support of the Bill of Rights. Toward the end of his life, Henry reversed his politics. He became alarmed at the radicalism and violence of the French Revolution and more closely aligned himself with Hamilton's Federalist Party.

PATRICK HENRY'S GOAL

◇◇◇◇◇◇◇◇◇◇◇◇◇◇◇◇◇

Because of rising tensions between the British army and the citizens of Boston, on March 23, 1775, the Virginia House of Burgesses convened to discuss security measures for their colony and whether or not they should send delegates to the upcoming Continental Congress. They knew that any extreme action would be considered treason, but the fiery congressional representative from Virginia, Patrick Henry, had no fear of this. He quickly proposed that Virginia draft a plan for assembling a force of armed militia.

Many of the conservative members of the House of Burgesses thought that to create a militia force would be going too far. Fearing defeat of his motion, Henry rose to defend his position. In one of the most inspirational speeches in American history, he vehemently argued that it was time to stand up to the British and prepare for conflict. His closing statement was the most iconic of the

Revolution. Referring to the behavior of the British army in Boston, he exclaimed:

"Our chains are forged! Their clanking may be heard on the plains of Boston! The war is inevitable and let it come… Why stand we here idle? What is it that Gentlemen wish? What would they have? Is life so dear, or peace so sweet, as to be purchased at the price of chains and slavery? Forbid it, Almighty God! I know not what course others may take; but as for me, give me liberty, or give me death!" [v]

Patrick Henry attained his goal. His motion for armed militia passed.

5

RESPECT YOUR PEOPLE

"I would sooner chop off my right hand than put it to the Constitution as it now stands."

—GEORGE MASON

This quote by Founding Father George Mason illustrates the bitter debate that took place among both Founders and followers over the acceptance and ratification of the U.S. Constitution. George Mason, who had authored the Virginia Declaration of Rights in June 1776, believed that the delegates of the U.S. Constitutional Convention were making a huge mistake in the fall of 1787. He believed the Constitution they had written granted too much power to the federal government and did not sufficiently guarantee the rights of the people.

Only four years prior to this Constitutional Convention, the nation had barely survived a bitter war of revolution, which Americans had entered into because of their anger toward the British government. Parliament and the king had ignored the colonists' rights as British subjects and oppressed them with unwanted taxes, interfered with their right to trial by jury, and forced them to quarter British troops in their homes. Now that the colonists had thrown off the yoke of the king, some, like Mason, feared that the new government, whose constitution had been written by a handful of men behind closed doors, might become another tyrant to rule over them.

Federalist Party leaders like Alexander Hamilton and James Madison, who supported the ratification of the Constitution, were convinced their new government would never become tyrannical. They had carefully framed the government to establish a balance of power between the executive, legislative, and judicial branches. Additionally, the Constitution implied that any powers not specifically given to the federal government were retained by the people and the states.

At the close of the Constitutional Convention, the Federalists won out over Anti-Federalists like George Mason, and on December 17, 1787, the Constitution was approved and sent to the states for ratification. But after it was distributed to the states, the people protested. They repeatedly asked an angry question: Why did the Constitution not include a bill of rights?

While he was helping Alexander Hamilton write *The Federalist Papers* to support ratification of the Constitution, James Madison realized something more was needed. He began to recognize the legitimacy of the people's request for a bill of rights. Madison knew that Americans were inherently suspicious of government and afraid that if their specific rights such as freedom of speech or the worship of God were not explicitly spelled out, even a balanced, republican form of government might one day become tyrannical and interfere with those sacred rights.

So Madison decided to honor the people's wishes and promised to lead the effort to adopt a bill of rights. His task proved challenging. Over two hundred amendments were proposed, most of which were for states' rights rather than individual rights. Thanks to Madison's leadership, these were finally pared down to twelve proposed constitutional amendments, each of which he made certain was written in language that ordinary people could understand and, if they wanted to, memorize. On December 15, 1791, the states ratified ten of these amendments, and today they comprise what we the people call the "Bill of Rights."

> "The equal rights of man, and the happiness of every individual, are now acknowledged to be the only legitimate objects of government."
>
> —THOMAS JEFFERSON

Three key actions for respecting your people

☞ Treat Them as Individuals

☞ Intellectually Challenge Them

☞ Honor Their Beliefs and Families

TREAT THEM AS INDIVIDUALS

There is nothing more impressive than a leader who knows every team member well. He or she knows not only each member's name and job function, but more importantly, he or she knows them personally. This is not difficult if your team is of reasonable size, so if this is your situation, do it!

If your team is too large to know everyone personally, make yourself available for meetings with small groups or individuals. Do your homework before these meetings occur. Know as much as possible about the team and the people you're going to meet with. Ask about their personal goals. Encourage them to talk about themselves. Listen. This will result in not only a more cohesive team, but also an increased environment of trust.

INTELLECTUALLY CHALLENGE THEM

To determine the best way to challenge your follow-ers intellectually, you must first consider the group's purpose and degree of congruity. Are you working exclusively with a team of writers on a monthly newslet-ter? Or with a wide range of skill sets (engineers, sales personnel, graphic artists) on a product integration project? How you challenge your followers will initially be a function of the team's composition and purpose.

Once you've considered the team's nature, look at

the competence and maturity level of individual team members. There are many tools (such as situational leadership theory) that are useful for assessing team members' competence and maturity. In addition to the maturity level of team members, project maturity (how far it has progressed) should also be considered. Tools for assessing project maturity are numerous and readily available. Once you've done your homework, you can figure out the best way to challenge your followers intellectually.

"To cherish and stimulate the activity of the human mind, by multiplying the objects of enterprise, is not among the least considerable of the expedients, by which the wealth of a nation may be promoted."

—ALEXANDER HAMILTON[III]

HAMILTON'S INTELLECTUAL CHALLENGE

◇◇◇◇◇◇◇◇◇◇◇◇◇◇◇◇◇◇

In late January 1791, the Senate approved Alexander Hamilton's bill for the establishment of a national bank. When the bill reached President George Washington for signature, he had only ten days to either approve it or issue a veto. Washington knew Secretary Hamilton's opinion, but he decided to ask Attorney General Edmund Randolph and Secretary of State Thomas Jefferson if they thought the bank was constitutional. They both provided written verdicts declaring that it was not, with Jefferson expressing his opinion that Hamilton's reasons for the bank were a perversion of the "necessary and proper" clause of the Constitution.

Washington rushed Randolph and Jefferson's verdicts to his secretary of the treasury for comment. Over the course of the next week, Hamilton wrote a nearly fifteen thousand–word manifesto that has been called "the most brilliant argument for a broad interpretation of the Constitution in American political literature."[iv] To liberate the government from a restrictive reading of the Constitution, Hamilton effectively argued that in its "implied powers" the government had the right to employ all means necessary to carry out powers specified in the Constitution.

Hamilton contended that a bank of the United States would enable the government to make good on four powers cited explicitly in the Constitution: the rights to collect taxes, borrow money, regulate trade among states, and support fleets and armies. In the end, Washington decided that Hamilton's intellectual argument overwhelmed Thomas Jefferson's and Edmund Randolph's opinions, and he approved the bill.

HONOR THEIR BELIEFS
AND FAMILIES

By honoring the beliefs, values, and families of your team members, you are not only demonstrating respect for your followers, but you are also treating them as individuals—and making friends. Becoming a friend to your followers can be much more rewarding than simply being their leader.

Find out what's important to your followers outside of the workplace. If you can do so, get to know their families. Be sensitive to the fact that your followers have individual needs that may revolve around their personal values, their religious beliefs, or their families. Do your best to respect and accommodate them!

"The happiest moments of my life have been the few which I have past [*sic*] at home in the bosom of my family."

—THOMAS JEFFERSON[V]

BIOGRAPHICAL NOTE
JAMES MADISON

....

James Madison, a wealthy landowner from Virginia, was a political theorist, a state legislator, a member of the Continental Congress, a member of the U.S. House of Representatives, secretary of state in the Jefferson administration, and the fourth president of the United States. He led the effort to draft the United States

Constitution in 1787, assisted Hamilton in the writing of *The Federalist Papers*, and led the effort to develop the Bill of Rights—earning the sobriquet "Father of the Bill of Rights." Although he was initially a Federalist, he later broke ranks with Alexander Hamilton and joined with Thomas Jefferson to become a cofounder of the Democratic-Republican Party. With Jefferson, he fought for a less centralized government and an agriculturally based economy. Along with Jefferson, he also opposed Hamilton's initiatives to establish a strong navy and a strong, permanent army. After he became president and led the nation through the War of 1812, Madison realized the value of having a strong military and embraced Hamilton's vision.

6

CONVEY AN INSPIRING VISION

On April 30, 1789, George Washington took office as the nation's first president. The man who would one day be eulogized as "first in war, first in peace, and first in the hearts of his countrymen" faced monumental problems as the executive of a fledgling nation. The government he would lead had a new, untried constitution (without, for the time being, a bill of rights), a new Congress, and a national economy that was in complete shambles. Of Washington's many troubles,

America's economy loomed the largest. The United States of America had no international credit, a worthless national currency, and no definitive means of taxation or raising revenue.

To address America's overwhelming fiscal problems, Washington turned to his most trusted advisor—the gifted thirty-four-year-old Alexander Hamilton—and appointed him as the first United States secretary of the treasury.

Hamilton, a true visionary, proved equal to the task. Even as a youth, he had possessed a good grasp of business and trade. When a young officer on Washington's staff, he continued to study international trade and finance. In his new role as secretary of the treasury, he immersed himself in scores of books on finance and banking. He sought the counsel of financial experts in America and studied the economic philosophies of luminaries such as Malachy Postlethwayt of Great Britain and Scottish economist Adam Smith. He researched European economies and banking systems, and quickly developed his vision for a robust American economy.

Hamilton had always been an advocate of a strong centralized government, and within months of taking charge at the Treasury Department in late 1790, he produced a forty-thousand-word report regarding the approach he would take to solving the most pressing of the nation's economic problems—the national debt and poor public credit. He soon followed up this erudite "Report on the Public Credit" with equally intellectual reports on the establishment of a national bank and the development of a manufacturing economy.

Brilliant though they were, Hamilton's plans for attaining his vision for a robust American economy were not universally supported. His concept of a national bank—the forerunner of today's Federal Reserve System—and a strong, central, industrial economy was opposed by other Founding Fathers such as Thomas Jefferson and James Madison. Madison had previously been a member of Hamilton's Federalist Party, but he disagreed with Hamilton on financial issues, and it was the latter's proposal of a national bank that caused Madison to break with his former ally.

Hamilton and his Federalist Party continued to call for a strong national government that promoted economic growth and friendly relations with Great Britain. Jefferson formed an opposing political party, the Democratic-Republicans, who offered a different vision of America's future—that of strong state governments, an agrarian economy, and friendly relations with France.

Although both political parties would die out by the 1820s, their competing visions of governmental power and economy would battle each other for decades. Their contest was not resolved until the American Civil War, when Hamilton's vision prevailed.

"As to whatever may depend on enterprise, we [Americans] need not fear to be outdone by any people on earth. It may almost be said that enterprise is our element."

—ALEXANDER HAMILTON[1]

Three key actions for conveying an inspiring vision

☞ See the Future

☞ Describe Your Vision

☞ Turn Followers into Leaders

{ SEE THE FUTURE

Your vision is your description of the future. It is your dream. Even though it might represent a huge change from the status quo, it should be described as briefly and simply as possible. Have a picture in your mind that can easily be transferred to others. For an army commander, it might be "to see our flag on that hill." For an athlete, it might be "to hold the first place trophy." For Alexander Hamilton, it was a "healthy American economy." For you, it might be "improved health care in our community." As Martin Luther King Jr. demonstrated at the Lincoln Memorial on August 28, 1963, statements about our dreams for the future can be one of the most important accomplishments of our lifetime.

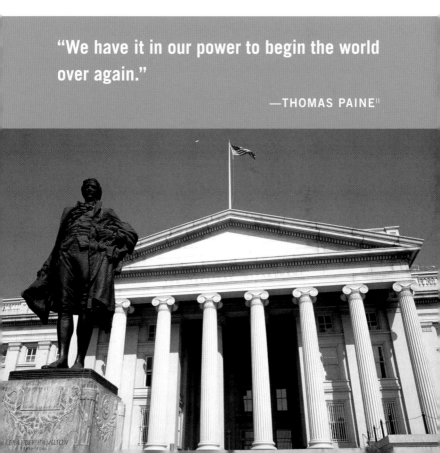

"We have it in our power to begin the world over again."

—THOMAS PAINE[11]

{ DESCRIBE YOUR VISION

Hamilton's 1790 report on the public credit and his subsequent reports on a national bank and a manufacturing-based economy have been called "the most important and influential state papers of their time" and remain among "the most brilliant government reports in American history."[iii] With them, Hamilton provided America an effective description of how to accomplish his vision.

Your vision may not be as all-encompassing as

Hamilton's, but you must nevertheless effectively articulate it to your followers. This is frequently done by one or more vision statements. Vision statements are, typically, short phrases or sentences that describe your dream for the future. By developing vision statements, you clarify your beliefs and governing principles of your organization or team.

You should develop a vision statement that is brief, clear, challenging, and appropriate. If your statement is not brief, it will be easily forgotten. If it is not clear, your followers may get sidetracked. If it is not challenging, it may be disregarded. If it is not appropriate, it will be impossible to motivate followers to embrace it.

"I hope, some day or another, we shall become a storehouse and granary for the world."

—GEORGE WASHINGTON[IV]

TURN FOLLOWERS INTO LEADERS

After you've described a succinct vision, your next job as an effective leader is to inspire your followers to take ownership and pursue it. You want them to become leaders in your cause. Everyone might agree that a new community medical center is a great idea, but if they do not see the connection between themselves and your vision, you have failed.

The art of turning followers into leaders encompasses more than the development of vision statements. You must treat your followers as leaders in order to develop leaders. This process involves virtually every skill discussed in this book. Moral integrity inspires honesty and trust. Defining "the most important thing" and demonstrating your personal commitment inspires team commitment. By establishing clear goals and showing respect for your people, you in turn earn their respect. Followers who respect a leader want to emulate that leader.

"The fabric of American empire ought to rest on the solid basis of the consent of the people. The streams of national power ought to flow from that pure, original fountain of all legitimate authority."

—ALEXANDER HAMILTON[v]

JOHN STARK'S VISION

◇◇◇◇◇◇◇◇◇◇◇◇◇◇◇

Colonel John Stark, as a Revolutionary War commander of New England militia, had one rare and priceless quality: he knew the limitations of his men. They had very little military training, were generally undisciplined, and were very cautious in battle. But Stark was the sort of officer who knew how to lead inexperienced troops, and when he marched his force up against a fort manned by British soldiers and their German mercenaries, he did not hesitate to order an attack. He knew how to challenge and inspire his men, and when forming for the assault he called out to them: "Yonder are the Hessians! They were bought for seven pounds and ten pence a man. Are you worth more? Prove it! Tonight the American flag floats from yonder hill or Molly Stark sleeps a widow!"[vi] Stark led his men in a charge on the fort and overwhelmed its defenders.

BIOGRAPHICAL NOTE
JOHN ADAMS

....

John Adams, a prominent resident of Massachusetts, was a leading political theorist, lawyer, statesman, and diplomat. He played an important role in persuading Congress to declare independence from Great Britain and assisted Thomas Jefferson in drafting the Declaration of Independence. Adams, Benjamin Franklin, and John Jay negotiated the Treaty of Paris, which formally ended the American Revolutionary War on September 3, 1783. He was vice president under George Washington from 1789 to 1797, and the second president of the United States from 1797 to 1801. The only member of the Federalist Party to ever become president, he was not on friendly terms with the party founder, Hamilton. He was a longtime political rival of Thomas

Jefferson, and lost his bid for reelection to him in 1800. Like Hamilton, Adams had a strong posture on national defense and was often called the Father of the American Navy. Both Adams and Jefferson died on July 4, 1826, fifty years to the day after signing the Declaration of Independence.

7

BE A MENTOR

Benjamin Franklin stood up to deliver his closing arguments on the last day of the Constitutional Convention. At eighty-one, Franklin was by far the oldest man in the room—twenty-six years older than George Washington, and fifty years older than Alexander Hamilton. He was one of only six men present who had signed the Declaration of Independence eleven years earlier, and the only representative present of the three ministers who had signed the Treaty of Paris in 1783. As the crafty American ambassador to France during the Revolution, he had been largely responsible for France's generous support during the war.

Franklin had earned his right to speak, and a respectful silence fell among the delegates. But Benjamin Franklin's voice was too weak to deliver his prepared remarks, so he asked his friend and fellow delegate from Pennsylvania, James Wilson, to read his prepared speech aloud. As Franklin gazed steadily across the assembly, his words filled the room.

"Mr. President: I confess that I do not entirely approve of this Constitution at present, but Sir, I am not sure I shall never approve it: For having lived long, I have experienced many Instances of being oblig'd, by better Information or fuller Consideration, to change Opinions even on important Subjects, which I once thought right, but found to be otherwise. It is therefore that the older I grow the

more apt I am to doubt my own Judgment, and to pay more Respect to the Judgment of others…"[i]

James Wilson continued the ten-minute speech, expressing Franklin's amazement that in spite of its faults the new constitution approached "so near to Perfection as it does." He implored each delegate to put aside his reservations and "doubt a little of his own Infallibility, and [in order] to make manifest our Unanimity, put his Name to this instrument."

Franklin had the reputation of being early America's Renaissance man and was world-renowned as a scientist, inventor, diplomat, author, newspaper editor, printer, politician, political theorist, postmaster, statesman, and civic activist. Having lived for years in England, he had surprised everyone in 1775 when he dropped his longstanding loyalty to the king and returned to America. He signed the Declaration of Independence and was later sent to France to serve as his nation's ambassador. While living in Paris, the seventy-year-old Franklin became the darling of French society.

Franklin was a mentor not only to his fellow Founders, but to all Americans. From 1732 to 1758, he had delighted the public with his popular *Poor Richard's Almanack*, which was filled with practical information and his incomparable witticisms. Although Franklin had developed many useful inventions, he never patented them. He gave his reasons in his famous autobiography, where he said, "As we enjoy great advantages from the inventions of others, we should be glad of an opportunity to serve others by any invention of ours; and this we should do freely and generously..."[ii]

In spite of all his accomplishments, Benjamin Franklin never lost his sense of humility. Even though he had lingering doubts about the new constitution, he decided that he was "not sure that it is not the best" that could be attained. By the end of the day, thirty-nine of the fifty-five delegates signed the

Constitution, and Benjamin Franklin's signature was proudly among them.

~~~~~~~~~

Three key actions for being a mentor

☞ Be Humble

☞ Keep Learning

☞ Share Knowledge

} BE HUMBLE

If you are convinced that you know it all, how will you ever learn anything? If anyone in his generation could claim to have wisdom, it would have been Benjamin Franklin. But toward the end of his life, in the presence of an assembly of younger men, Franklin admitted that although he had his doubts about the new constitution, he might be wrong.

Always have the attitude that "I will learn something new today." Be "quick to listen and slow to speak."[iii] Ask people for their opinions. Do not be afraid to admit it when you are uncertain of an answer. Your humility will pay off as you gain the respect of your followers, while learning what you need to know.

"The better any man is, the lower thoughts he has of himself."

—JAMES MADISON[IV]

{ KEEP LEARNING

Alexander Hamilton realized that he did not know as much as he needed to about economics and finance when he became secretary of the treasury. He immersed himself in scores of books on the subjects of banking, international trade, public debt, credit, foreign-exchange rates, taxation, and manufacturing. To broaden his understanding of world commerce, he researched peripherally related subjects such as politics, government, geography, and philosophy.

He learned what he could about financial matters from the great authors of his age, including Hume, Montesquieu, and Hobbes. He studied the Bank of England and the French Council of Commerce. He sought out his own mentors, notable men of business such as "the financier of the Revolution,"[v] Robert Morris.

In the age of instant information, you can do even better than Hamilton. Learn your subject!

"In a multitude of counselors there is the best chance for honesty, if not wisdom."

—JAMES MADISON[vi]

SHARE KNOWLEDGE

As a leader, make it a point to become a mentor to others. This will benefit you as well as your followers, because to teach others, you have to learn your subject well. By answering followers' questions, you will gain insight you would not otherwise have acquired.

Look for opportune moments to share what you've learned. Talk to your followers in informal settings. Give presentations. Offer to speak at seminars. Get published!

If you become known as a guru, you will be challenged by an increasing number of people and more difficult questions. And you will learn even more.

But never forget the first action item: remain humble.

"We are sent here to consult, not to contend with each other."

—BENJAMIN FRANKLIN[VII]

JOHN ADAMS SHARING KNOWLEDGE

◇◇◇◇◇◇◇◇◇◇◇◇◇◇◇◇◇◇

John Adams was one of the first of the Founding Fathers to encourage the American colonies' movement toward independence from Great Britain. He was an outspoken critic of the king's Stamp Act in 1765—ten years before the American Revolutionary War began. Adams became one of America's most capable statesmen, lawyers, authors, and diplomats. An eloquent writer, he was one of five delegates appointed by the Second Continental Congress to pen the first draft of the Declaration of Independence. Although Thomas Jefferson wanted Adams to take the lead, Adams convinced the committee to give the responsibility to Jefferson.

Adams retained the high esteem of the other Founding Fathers throughout the Revolutionary War. Seven years before the adoption of the revised United States Constitution, John Adams was asked to write the first draft of the Constitution of the Commonwealth of

Massachusetts. The Massachusetts Constitution became effective on October 25, 1780, and endures as the world's oldest functioning written constitution. Organized into a structure of chapters, sections, and articles, Adams's document served as a model for the United States Constitution that was approved on September 17, 1787.

BIOGRAPHICAL NOTE
BENJAMIN FRANKLIN

....

Benjamin Franklin, a resident of Massachusetts, earned the title of "The First American" as a result of his role as the senior statesman of the First and Second Continental Congresses, drafter of the Articles of Confederation, Ambassador to France during the Revolutionary War, signer of both the Declaration of Independence and the final U.S. Constitution, and cosigner of the Treaty of Paris, which ended the

American Revolutionary War. Franklin was a world-renowned author, printer, scientist, inventor, and political theorist. He is famous for his experiments verifying that lightning is actually electricity and for his many inventions, including the Franklin stove, lightning rod, and bifocal glasses. In addition to being first minister to France, he was first minister to Sweden and the first postmaster general of the United States. Toward the end of his life, he freed his slaves and became, like fellow Founder Alexander Hamilton, a prominent abolitionist.

EPILOGUE

Seven months before the British formally conceded America's independence at the Treaty of Paris in 1783, General George Washington marveled at what his generation had accomplished in its victory over the king's military forces in America:

It will not be believed that such a force as Great Britain has employed for eight years in this Country could be baffled in their

plan of Subjugating it by numbers infinitely less—composed of Men oftentimes half starved—always in Rags—without pay—& experiencing, at times, every species of distress which human nature is capable of undergoing.[i]

The victory, despite overwhelming odds, was not only a result of the leadership of a few men we refer to as the Founding Fathers, but also of the leadership they instilled in their followers. During the course of the Revolution, both Founders and followers had truly encouraged one another to "higher levels of morality and motivation."[ii]

The Founders were well read in the teachings of the ancient Greek and Roman philosophers and statesmen such as Plato, Aristotle, and Cicero. They were animated by contemporary enlightenment thinkers such as Thomas Hobbes, John Locke, Voltaire, Montesquieu, and Jean-Jacques Rousseau. Consequently, even though leadership theory did not emerge as a unique field of investigation until the mid-nineteenth century, in their studies the Founders had prepared themselves well to become revolutionary leaders.

The ultimate secret of the Founding Fathers was that in adopting the cause of establishing a republic based on the rights of the common man, they discovered and defined "the right thing to do." No matter what their leadership skills may have been, how passionately they spoke, how eloquently they wrote, how much they threw themselves into their cause—if their cause had not been right, and if it had not resonated with their followers, they would probably have failed. George Washington would have never had occasion to later recall "you might have tracked the army from White Marsh to Valley Forge by the blood on their feet."[iii]

Today we honor the Founding Fathers for their courage, magnificent works, and brilliant leadership. But the Founders themselves refused to take complete credit for their success. This is evidenced in the writings of virtually all of them, and their common belief was eloquently summarized in the following statement by the orphaned immigrant from the Caribbean who arrived in America just in time for the Revolution:

"The sacred rights of mankind are not to be rummaged for, among old parchments, or musty records. They are written, as with a sun beam, in the whole volume of human nature, by the hand of the Divinity itself, and can never be erased or obscured by mortal power."

—ALEXANDER HAMILTON[IV]

John Penn   John Hancock   John Hart
Wm Floyd   Wm Paca

Geo Read   Wm Hooper   Saml Adams
Step Hopkins   Thos Nelson jr   Geo Clymer
Charles Carroll of Carrollton   Elbridge Gerry
Tho. M:Kean   Roger Sherman   Saml Huntington
Wm Whipple of.   Thomas Lynch Junr
Geo Taylor   Josiah Bartlett   Benjⁿ Franklin
Wm Williams   Rich Stockton
                                    John Morton
Oliver Wolcott   Jno Witherspoon le Geo. Ross
Thos Stone   Samuel Chase   Robt Treat Paine
George Wythe   Matthew Thornton
Fran^s Lewis   Th Jefferson   Benj^a Harrison
Lewis Morris   Abra Clark   Phil. Livingston
                                    Casar Rodney
Arthur Middleton   Fras Hopkinson
Geo Walton   Carter Braxton   James Wilson
Richard Henry Lee   Thos Heyward Junr
Benjamin Rush   John Adams   Robt Morris
Lyman Hall   Joseph Hewes   Button Gwinnett
Francis Lightfoot Lee
William Ellery   Edward Rutledge   Ja^s Smith

ENDNOTES

Introduction

[i]   John Adams to H. Niles, February 13, 1818, Teaching AmericanHistory.org, accessed September 7, 2016, http://teachingamericanhistory.org/library/document/john-adams-to-h-niles/.

[ii]   Timothy O'Connell and Brent Cuthbertson, *Group Dynamics in Recreation and Leisure* (Champaign: Human Kinetics: 2009), 115.

Chapter One

[i]   Ron Chernow, *Alexander Hamilton* (New York: Penguin Books, 2005), 37.

[ii] Buckner F. Melton, ed., *The Quotable Founding Fathers* (Washington, DC: Potomac Books, 2004), 31.

[iii] Ibid., 21.

[iv] Alexander Hamilton to Edward Stevens, November 11, 1769, National Archives, accessed September 7, 2016, http://founders.archives.gov/documents/Hamilton/01-01 -02-0002.

[v]   George Bancroft, *History of the United States of America*, vol. 4, 1889 (New York: D. Appleton and Company, 1886), 293.

Chapter Two

[i]   Andrew Jackson O'Shaughnessy, *The Men Who Lost America* (New Haven: Yale University Press, 2013), 85.

[ii] John Adams to Abigail Adams, June 11, 1775, National Archives, accessed September 7, 2016, http://founders .archives.gov/documents/Adams/04-01-02-0146.

iii   Buckner F. Melton, ed., *The Quotable Founding Fathers* (Washington, DC: Potomac Books, 2004), 133.

iv   From Thomas Jefferson to Edward Carrington, 16 January 1787, National Archives, accessed September 7, 2016, https://founders.archives.gov/documents/Jefferson/01-11-02-0047.

v   Thomas Jefferson to Peter Carr, August 19, 1785, Henry Stephens Randall, *The Life of Thomas Jefferson*, vol. 1, 1858 (New York: Derby & Jackson, 1858), 436.

vi   George Washington, *Maxims of Washington*, ed. John Frederick Schroeder (New York: D. Appleton and Company, 1854), 79.

Chapter Three

i   Benjamin Franklin, *The Works of Benjamin Franklin*, ed. Jared Sparks (Boston: Charles Tappan, 1844), 408.

ii   David McCullough, *1776* (New York: Simon & Schuster, 2005), 159.

iii   Thomas Jefferson, *The Jeffersonian Cyclopedia*, ed. John P Foley (New York: Funk & Wagnalls Company, 1900), 243.

Chapter Four

[i]   John R. Vile, *The Constitutional Convention of 1787* (Santa Barbara: ABC-CLIO, 2005), 20.

[ii]   Ibid., 916.

[iii] Alexander Hamilton, "Federalist #1," *The Federalist Papers*, The Avalon Project, accessed September 7, 2016, http://avalon.law.yale.edu/18th_century/fed01.asp.

[iv]   Benjamin Franklin, *The Works of Benjamin Franklin*, ed. Jared Sparks (Boston: Charles Tappan, 1844), 358.

[v]   Robert C. Etheredge, *The American Challenge* (Orinda: MiraVista Press, 2011), 276.

Chapter Five

[i]   Fred Rodell, *55 Men: The Story of the Constitution* (Harrisburg: Stackpole Books, 1936), 193.

[ii]   Thomas Jefferson, *The Jeffersonian Cyclopedia*, ed. John P Foley (New York: Funk & Wagnalls Company, 1900), 388.

[iii] Cynthia Clark Northrup, *The American Economy: A Historical Encyclopedia* (Santa Barbara: ABC-CLIO, 2003), 523.

iv   Ron Chernow, *Alexander Hamilton* (New York: Penguin Books, 2005), 354.

v   Thomas Jefferson to Francis Willis, Jr., April 18, 1790, National Archives, accessed September 7, 2016, http://founders.archives.gov/documents/Jefferson/01-16-02-0203.

Chapter Six

i   John C. Miller, *Alexander Hamilton and the Growth of the New Nation* (New Brunswick: Transaction Publishers, 2004), 428.

ii   Daniel K. Richter, *Before the Revolution* (Cambridge: The Belknap Press, 2011), 3.

iii   Darren Staloff, *Hamilton, Adams, Jefferson: The Politics of Enlightenment and the American Founding* (New York: Hill and Wang, 2007), 91.

iv   Buckner F. Melton, ed., *The Quotable Founding Fathers* (Washington, DC: Potomac Books, 2004), 6.

v   Alexander Hamilton, "Federalist #22," *The Federalist Papers*, The Avalon Project, accessed July 19, 2018, http://avalon.law.yale.edu/18th_century/fed22.asp.

vi John C. Fredriksen, *American Military Leaders* (Santa Barbara: ABC-CLIO, 1999), 1:768.

Chapter Seven

i Tobias George Smollett, *The Critical Review: Or, Annals of Literature*, vol. 9 (London: J. Mawman, 1807), 353.

ii Benjamin Franklin, *The Autobiography of Benjamin Franklin* (Philadelphia: J.B. Lippincott, 1868), 55.

iii James 1:19.

iv James Madison, *The Papers of James Madison* , vol. 1, ed. William T. Hutchinson and William M. E. Rachal (Chicago: University of Chicago Press, 1962), 52.

v Charles Rappleye, *Robert Morris: Financier of the American Revolution* (New York: Simon & Schuster, 2010), 158.

vi Buckner F. Melton, ed., *The Quotable Founding Fathers*, (Washington, DC: Potomac Books, 2004), 3.

vii Benjamin Franklin, *The Political Thought of Benjamin Franklin*, ed. Ralph Ketcham (Indianapolis: Hackett Publishing Company, 2003), 392.

Epilogue

i   George Washington to Nathanael Greene, February 6, 1783, National Archives, accessed September 7, 2016, http://founders.archives.gov/documents/Washington/99-01-02-10582.

ii   James MacGregor Burns, *Leadership* (New York: Harper & Row, 1978), 20.

iii   John E. Ferling, *The First of Men: A Life of George Washington* (Oxford: Oxford University Press, 2010), 221.

iv   Scott J. Hammond, Kevin R. Hardwick, and Howard Leslie Lubert, eds., *Classics of American Political and Constitutional Thought*, vol. 1 (Indianapolis: Hackett Publishing Company, 2007), 261.

ABOUT THE AUTHOR

GORDON LEIDNER is the author of the book *The Founding Fathers: Quotes, Quips, and Speeches* as well as greatamericanhistory.net, a popular history website for students and educators. He has written numerous books and articles about American history, including analyses of Abraham Lincoln's transformational leadership skills for academic journals.

He received an MGA in applied management at the University of Maryland University College. He has more than thirty years of engineering and management experience in the IT and aerospace industries and is a registered Project Management Professional (PMP).

EXCLUSIVELY
AVAILABLE ON
SIMPLETRUTHS.COM

Need a training framework?
Engage your team with discussion guides and PowerPoints for training events or meetings.

Want your own branded editions?
Express gratitude, appreciation, and instill positive perceptions to staff or clients by adding your organization's logo to your edition of the book.

Add a supplemental visual experience
to any meeting, training, or event.

Contact us for special corporate discounts!
(800) 900-3427 x247 or
simpletruths@sourcebooks.com

LOVED WHAT YOU READ AND WANT MORE?

Sign up today and be the FIRST to receive advance copies of Simple Truths® NEW releases written and signed by expert authors. Enjoy a complete package of supplemental materials that can help you host or lead a successful event. This high-value program will uplift you to be the best version of yourself!

— SIMPLE TRUTHS —
ELITE CLUB

ONE MONTH. ONE BOOK. ONE HOUR.

Your monthly dose of motivation, inspiration, and personal growth.